*Everybody's Favorite Series No. 250*

Trade Mark

# *Everybody's Favorite Piano Pieces For Children Book 2*

ISBN: 978-0-8256-1815-4

**HAL•LEONARD®**

Visit Hal Leonard Online at
**www.halleonard.com**

Contact us:
**Hal Leonard**
7777 West Bluemound Road
Milwaukee, WI 53213
Email: info@halleonard.com

In Europe, contact:
**Hal Leonard Europe Limited**
42 Wigmore Street
Marylebone, London, W1U 2RY
Email: info@halleonardeurope.com

In Australia, contact:
**Hal Leonard Australia Pty. Ltd.**
4 Lentara Court
Cheltenham, Victoria, 3192 Australia
Email: info@halleonard.com.au

# PIANO PIECES FOR CHILDREN 2

## COMPOSERS' INDEX

# FOLK TUNES

# PIANO PIECES FOR CHILDREN 2

## CONTENTS

# Raindrops

Grade I

Jacob Schmitt
(1803–1853)

# Walking

Grade I

Anton Diabelli
(1781–1858)

# Bourée

Grade I

Johann Sebastian Bach
(1685–1750)

**Allegro**

# Air

Grade I

Wilhelm Friedemann Bach
(1710–1784)

# Red River Valley

Grade I

American Cowboy Song

# She'll Be Comin' Round the Mountain

Grade I

American Folk Song

# Little Song

Grade I

Cornelius Gurlitt
(1820–1901)

# America, the Beautiful

Grade I

Samuel A. Ward

# Swing Low, Sweet Chariot

Grade I

African-American Spiritual

Chorus

# The Cuckoo

Grade I

August Eberhard Müller
(1767–1817)

# Bourée

Grade I

Johann Krieger
(1651–1735)

# Sonatina

Grade I

Albert Biehl
(1835–1899)

**Allegro moderato**

# When Johnny Comes Marching Home

Grade I

American Folk Song

**Lively march tempo**

# Yankee Doodle

Grade I

American Folk Song

**Lively**

# Britannia, the Gem of the Ocean

Grade I

English Anthem

# Two Minuets

(from *The Notebook for Nannerl*)

Leopold Mozart
(1719–1787)

Grade I

## I.

## II.

# Moscow Nights

Grade I

Russian Folk Song

# Beautiful Heaven
### (Cielito Lindo)

Grade I

Mexican Folk Song

# New World Symphony
## (Largo)

Grade I

Anton Dvořák
(1841–1904)

# Piano Concerto

## (Theme)

Grade I

Edvard Grieg
(1843–1907)

# Minuet

## (from *The Little Notebook of Anna Magdalena Bach*)

Grade I

Johann Sebastian Bach
(1685–1750)

# March
### (from *The Little Notebook of Anna Magdalena Bach*)

Grade I

Johann Sebastian Bach
(1685–1750)

# Symphony No. 1
## (Finale)

Grade I

Johannes Brahms
(1833–1897)

**Moderate, steady motion**

# Symphony No. 7
### (Second Movement)

Grade I

Ludwig van Beethoven
(1770–1827)

**Allegretto**

# My Bonnie

Grade I

Scottish Folk Song

# Toyland

(from *Babes in Toyland*)

Grade I

Victor Herbert
(1833–1897)

**Slowly, dreamily**

# Alouette

Grade I

French-Canadian Folk Song

# To a Wild Rose

Grade I

Edward MacDowell
(1861–1908)

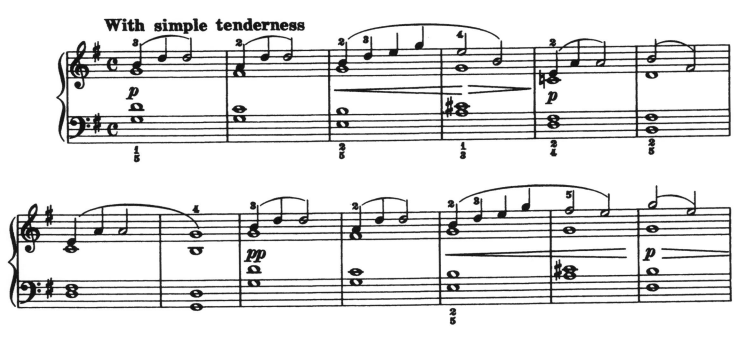

# Arietta

Grade I

Wolfgang Amadeus Mozart
(1756–1791)

# Waltz

Grade I

Franz Schubert
(1797–1828)

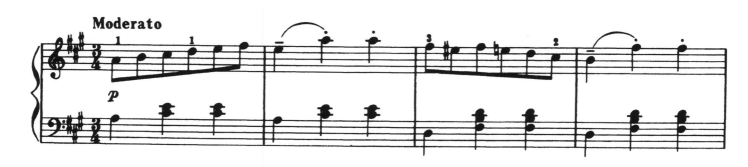

# Minuet

Grade I

Domenico Scarlatti
(1685–1757)

# Bourée

Grade I

George Frideric Handel
(1685–1759)

Animato

# Scottish Dance

Grade II

Friedrich Kuhlau
(1786–1832)

# Hide and Seek

Grade II

Robert Schumann
(1810–1856)

# German Dance

Grade II

Franz Joseph Haydn
(1732–1809)

# Chorale

Grade II

Robert Schumann
(1810–1856)

# Caprice No. 24

Grade II

Niccolò Paganini
(1782–1840)

# My Heart at Thy Sweet Voice

Grade II

Camille Saint-Saëns
(1835–1921)

**Moderately slow**

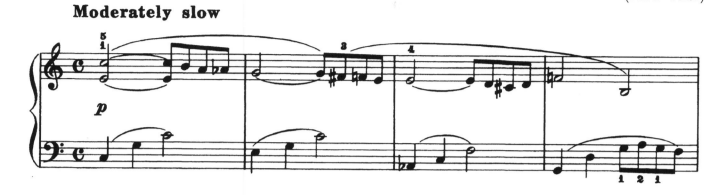

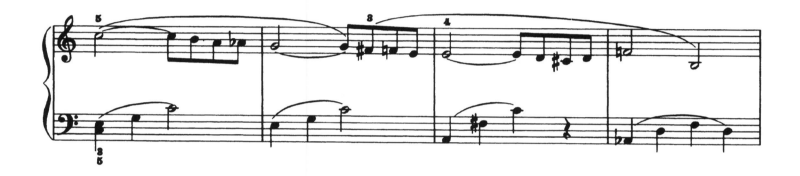

# Allegretto Scherzando

Grade II

Carl Phillip Emanuel Bach
(1714–1788)

# Prelude No. 2
### (from *Twelve Little Preludes*)

Grade II

Johann Sebastian Bach
(1685–1750)

**Allegro non troppo**

# Moonlight Sonata

## (Adagio)

Grade II

Ludwig van Beethoven
(1770–1827)

# Theme from Variations in A

Grade II

Wolfgang Amadeus Mozart
(1756–1791)

# Minuet in F

Grade II

Wolfgang Amadeus Mozart
(1756–1791)

# Zerlina's Song

(from *Don Giovanni*)

Grade II

Wolfgang Amadeus Mozart
(1756–1791)

# Minuet

Grade II

Johann Sebastian Bach
(1685–1750)

# Bagatelle

Grade II

Robert Schumann
(1810–1856)

# Hungarian Dance No. 4

Grade II

Johannes Brahms
(1833–1897)

# Piano Concerto No. 21
## (Andante)

Grade II

Wolfgang Amadeus Mozart
(1756–1791)

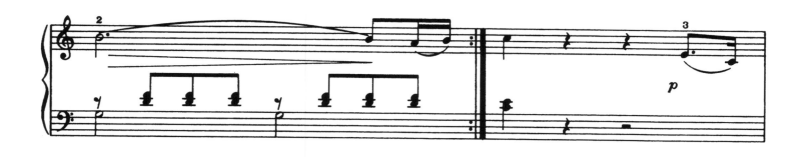

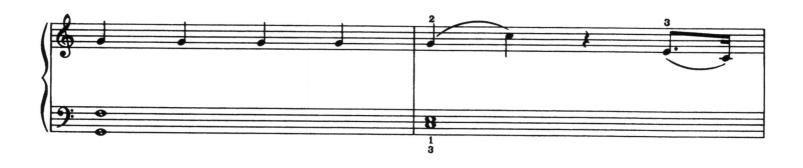

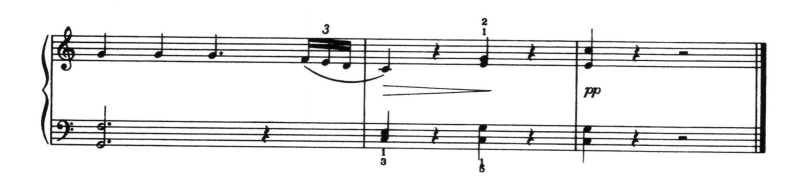

# Eroica Symphony
## (Theme)

Grade II

Ludwig van Beethoven
(1770–1827)

# Farandole

(from *L'Arlesienne Suite No. 2*)

Grade II

Georges Bizet
(1838–1875)

# The Doll's Complaint

Grade II

César Franck
(1822–1890)

# Mighty Lak' a Rose

Grade II

Ethelbert Nevin
(1862–1901)

**Slowly and gently**

*D.C. al Fine*

# Symphony No. 5
## (Second Movement)

Grade II

Peter Ilyich Tchaikovsky
(1840–1893)

**Slowly**

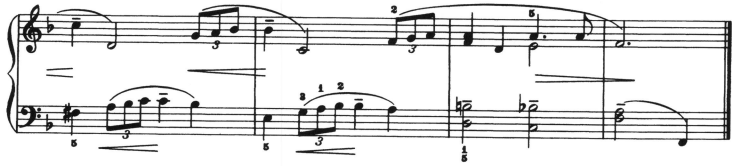

# Rondo alla Turca

Grade II

Wolfgang Amadeus Mozart
(1756–1791)

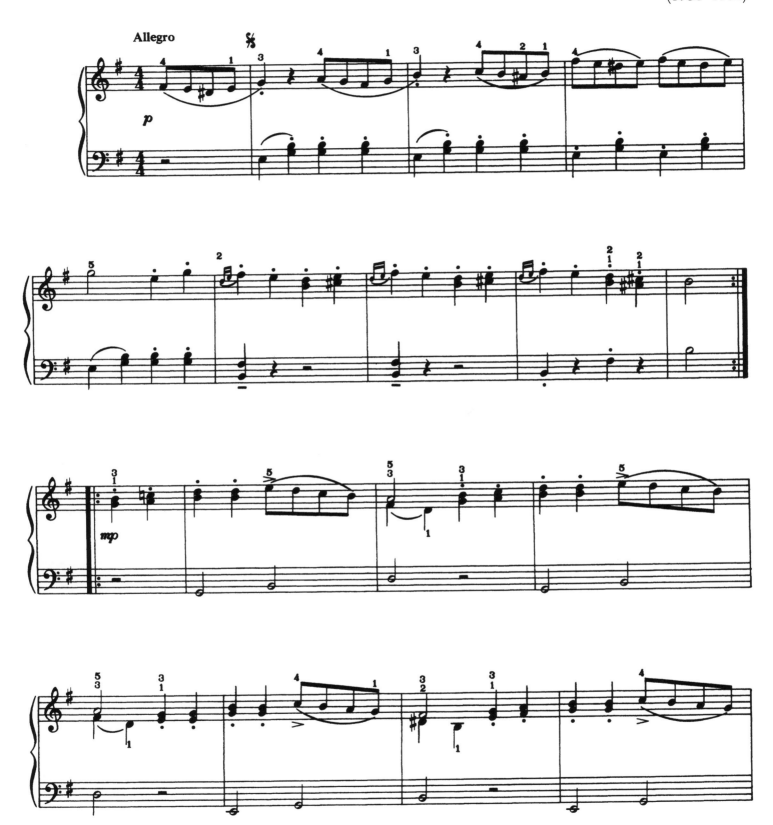

# Symphony No. 9
## (Ode to Joy)

Grade II

Ludwig van Beethoven
(1770–1827)

# A Musical Joke

Grade II

Wolfgang Amadeus Mozart
(1756–1791)

# Sleepers Awake

Grade II

Johann Sebastian Bach
(1685–1750)

# Gavotte

(from *French Suite No. 5*)

Grade II

Johann Sebastian Bach
(1685–1750)

# Minuet
### (from *Sonata in G Major*)

Grade II

Ludwig van Beethoven
(1770–1827)

# Polonaise

Grade II

Johann Sebastian Bach
(1685–1750)

# Rondino

Grade II

Anton Diabelli
(1781–1858)

# Dawn

Grade II

Ruggiero Leoncavallo
(1857–1919)

**Freely moving**

# Nocturne

Grade II

Frédéric Chopin
(1810–1849)

**Moderately**

# Studio

Grade II

Johann Christoph Friedrich Bach
(1732–1795)

# Capriccio Italien

Grade II

Peter Ilyich Tchaikovsky
(1840–1893)

# Scheherezade

Grade III

Nikolai Rimsky-Korsakov
(1844–1908)

# Andante Cantabile

Grade III

Peter Ilyich Tchaikovsky
(1840–1893)

# Give Me Your Hand

(from *Don Giovanni*)

Grade III

Wolfgang Amadeus Mozart
(1756–1791)

**Comfortable walking tempo**

# Toreador Song

(from *Carmen*)

Grade III

Georges Bizet
(1838–1875)

**Moderately, with vigor**

# Gavotte

(from *Violin Sonata No. 6*)

Grade III

Johann Sebastian Bach
(1685–1750)

**Graceful walking tempo**

# Piano Concerto No. 3
(First Movement)

Grade III

Ludwig van Beethoven
(1770–1827)

**Lively**

# Loch Lomond

Grade III

Scottish Folk Song

# Fascination

Grade III

Filippo D. Marchetti

# Chicken Reel

Grade III

American Fiddle Tune

# Polka

Grade III

Mikhail Glinka
(1804–1857)

# Waltz Medley

Grade III

Johann Strauss
(1804–1849)

**Moderately**

**Lively**

# Sheep May Safely Graze

(from *Birthday Cantata*)

Grade III

Johann Sebastian Bach
(1685–1750)

# The Bell Song

## (from *Lakmé*)

Grade III

Léo Delibes
(1836–1891)

**Very lively**

# Old French Song

Grade III

Peter Ilyich Tchaikovsky
(1840–1893)

# Fantasie-Impromptu
## (Cantabile)

Grade III

Frédéric Chopin
(1810–1849)

# Etude

Grade III

Frédéric Chopin
(1810–1849)

Moderato

# Songs My Mother Taught Me

Grade III

Antonín Dvořák
(1841–1904)

Andante con moto

# Nocturne

(from *A Midsummer Night's Dream*)

Grade III

Felix Mendelssohn
(1809–1847)

# Piano Concerto No. 1
## (First Movement)

Grade III

Peter Ilyich Tchaikovsky
(1840–1893)

# Poem

Grade III

Zdenko Fibich
(1850–1900)

Slow Waltz Tempo

# The Mountainside Is Green

Grade III

German Folk Dance

# Parade of the Tin Soldiers

Grade III

Leon Jessel
(1871–1942)

**Lively and gracefully**

*D.C. al Fine*

# Goodbye

Grade III

Francesco Paolo Tosti
(1846–1916)

# Slavonic Dance No. 10

Grade III

Antonín Dvořák
(1841–1904)

# Polovetzian Dance

(from *Prince Igor*)

Grade III

Alexander Borodin
(1833–1887)

# Piano Concerto No.20
## (Romance)

Grade III

Wolfgang Amadeus Mozart
(1756–1791)

# Tambourin

Grade III

Jean Philippe Rameau
(1683–1764)

# Rondo

(from *Orchestral Suite No. 2*)

Grade III

Johann Sebastian Bach
(1685–1750)

# Badinerie

(from *Orchestral Suite No. 2*)

Grade III

Johann Sebastian Bach
(1685–1750)

# Sinfonia Concertante
## (Andante)

Grade III

Wolfgang Amadeus Mozart
(1756–1791)

# Three Gymnopédies

Grade III

Erik Satie
(1866–1925)

## I.

## II.

# III.

**Slowly and gravely**

# Symphony No. 3
## (Allegretto)

Grade IV

Johannes Brahms
(1833–1897)

# Chanson Triste
## (A Sad Song)

Grade IV

Peter Ilyich Tchaikovsky
(1840–1893)

# On Wings of Song

Grade IV

Felix Mendelssohn
(1809–1847)

# Romance

Grade IV

Anton Rubinstein
(1829–1894)

# Peasant Dance

Grade IV

Romanian Folk Tune

# Maple Leaf Rag

Grade IV

Scott Joplin
(1868–1917)

153

Trio

*mf*

*ff*

Fine

D.C. al Fine

# Rondo

(from *Sonata in C*)

Grade IV

Wolfgang Amadeus Mozart
(1756–1791)

# The Wild Horseman
### (from *Album for the Young*)

Grade IV

Robert Schumann
(1810–1856)

# Country Gardens

Grade IV

English Folk Dance

# Gavotte

Grade IV

François Joseph Gossec
(1734–1829)

# Waltz

Grade IV

Carl Maria von Weber<br>(1786–1826)

Trio

D.C. al Fine

# Liebestraum

Grade IV

Franz Liszt
(1811–1886)

# Confidence

Grade IV

Felix Mendelssohn
(1809–1847)

# Scherzo

Grade IV

Johann Nepomuk Hummel
(1778–1837)

# The Knitters

Grade IV

François Couperin
(1668–1733)

# Two-Part Invention No. 4

Grade IV

Johann Sebastian Bach
(1685–1750)

# Two-Part Invention No. 8

Grade IV

Johann Sebastian Bach
(1685–1750)

# Meditation

(from *Thais*)

Grade IV

Jules Massenet
(1842–1912)

# Rêverie

Grade IV

Claude Debussy
(1862–1918)

# Claire de Lune

Grade IV

Claude Debussy
(1862–1918)

**Slowly, with expression**

# PIANO PIECES FOR CHILDREN
## GLOSSARY FOR VOLUMES 1 AND 2
### MUSIC TERMS

**Adagio**  Slowly.

**Adagio non troppo**  Slowly, but not too much so.

**Accelerando** (abbr. **accel.**)  Growing faster.

**Accelerando poco a poco** (abbr. **accel. poco a poco**)  Growing faster little by little.

**Allargando**  Growing slower.

**Allegretto**  Moderately fast.

**Allegretto grazioso**  Moderately fast and gracefully.

**Allegretto grazioso e leggierissimo**  Moderately fast; gracefully and very lightly.

**Allegretto ma non troppo**  Moderately fast, but not too much so.

**Allegretto moderato**  A fast, but moderate, tempo.

**Allegretto scherzando**  Moderately fast and playfully.

**Allegretto tranquillo**  Moderately fast and calmly.

**Allegro**  Quickly.

**Allegro agitato**  Quickly and excitedly.

**Allegro con brio**  Quickly and spiritedly.

**Allegro deciso**  Quickly and energetically.

**Allegro giocoso**  Quickly and merrily.

**Allegro moderato**  A quick, but moderate, tempo.

**Allegro non troppo**  Quickly, but not too much so.

**Allegro scherzando**  Quickly and playfully.

**Allegro tranquillo**  Quickly and calmly.

**Allegro vivace**  Quickly and spiritedly.

**Ancora tranquillo**  Calmly, as before.

**Andante**  Moderately slowly; a walking pace.

**Andante con moto**  Moderately slow, with movement.

**Andante espressivo**  Moderately slow and expressive.

**Andantino**  Moderately slow; a brisk walking pace.

**Animato**  Animatedly; with spirit.

**Appassionato**  Passionately; with feeling.

**Assai vivo**  Very lively and spirited.

**A tempo**  Return to the previous rate of speed.

**Ben cantando**  In a nice flowing style; as if well sung.

**Breve**  Short in duration.

**Brillante**  Brilliant; showy.

**Calando**  Growing softer and slower.

**Calmato**  Calmly.

**Cantabile** (or **cantando**)  As if sung.

**Canto marcato**  With the melody emphasized.

**Chorus**  The refrain of a song, usually repeated after each verse.

**Coda**  A passage of music played at the end of a piece. (See "Music Symbols")

**Con brio**  With spirit.

**Con espressione** (also **con espressivo;** abbr. **con espress.**)  With expression.

**Con forza**  Forcefully.

**Con grazia**  With grace.

**Con molto passione**  With great feeling.

**Con moto**  With speed and energetic movement.

**Con pedal** (abbr. **con ped.**)  With pedal; indicates that the right (sustain) pedal is to be pressed as needed. (See "Music Symbols")

**Crescendo** (abbr. **cresc.**)  Growing louder. (See "Music Symbols")

**Crescendo al diminuendo** (abbr. **cresc. al dim.**)  Grow louder then softer.

**Crescendo al forte** (abbr. **cresc. al _f_**)  Increase volume until loud.

**Crescendo e ritardando** (abbr. **cresc. e rit.**)  Growing louder and slower.

**Crescendo molto** (abbr. **cresc. molto**)  Growing much louder.

**Crescendo sempre** (abbr. **cresc. sempre** or **sempre cresc.**)  Growing louder throughout.

**D.C., D.C. al Coda, D.C. al Fine, D.S., D.S. al Coda, D.S. al Fine, D.% al Fine**  (See "Music Symbols")

**Delicatamente**  Delicately.

**Diminuendo** (abbr. **dim.**)  Growing softer. (See "Music Symbols")

**Diminuendo e poco ritardando** (abbr. **dim. e poco rit.**)  Growing softer and a little slower.

**Diminuendo e rallentando** (abbr. **dimin. e rallent.**)  Growing softer and ever slower.

**Diminuendo e ritardando** (abbr. **dim. e rit.**)  Growing softer and slower.

**Diminuendo molto** (abbr. **dim. molto**)  Growing much softer.

**Diminuendo sempre** (abbr. **dim. sempre**)  Growing softer throughout.

**Dolce**  Sweetly.

**Dolce e cantabile**  Sweetly; as if sung.

**Dolce e più lento**  Sweetly and even more slowly.

**Dolcissimo**  Very sweetly.

**Espressivo** (abbr. **espress.**)  Expressively; with feeling.

**Fine**  The end of a repeated passage or piece. (See "Music Symbols")

**Grazioso e leggiero**  Gracefully and lightly.

**Il bass leggiero**  A light and airy bass part.

**Il basso marcato**  A distinct and prominent bass part.

**Il basso sempre staccato**  A lightly accented bass part throughout; with each note lasting less than its full value.

**La melodia marcato**  A distinct and prominent melody part.

**Larghetto**  Slowly.

**Largo**  Very slow and stately.

**Legatissimo** (abbr. **legatiss.**)  Very smoothly, with each note lasting its full value.

**Legato**  Smoothly, with each note lasting its full value.

**Legato con grazia**  Smoothly and gracefully.

**Leggero ed animato**  Lightly and animatedly.

**Leggiero** (also **leggero;** abbr. **legg.**)  Lightly and airily.

**Lento**  Slowly.

**Lento, na non troppo**  Slowly, but not too much so.

**L.H.**  Use the left hand. (See also **R.H.**)

**Maestoso**  Majestically; with dignity.

**Mancando**  Fading away.

**Marcato**  Distinctly; with emphasis.

**Marcato il canto**  With the melody emphasized.

**Meno mosso**  Less rapidly.

**Meno forte**  Less loudly.

**Misterioso**  Mysteriously.

**Moderato**  Moderately fast.

**Moderato assai**  Moderately fast throughout.

**Moderato e cantando**  Moderately fast and flowing.

**Molto cantabile**  As if sung freely.

**Molto e tranquillo**  Very calmly.

**Molto più lento capriccio** Much more slowly, as desired.

**Molto ritardando** (abbr. **molto ritard.** or **molto rit.**) Growing very much slower.

**Molto ritenuto** (abbr. **molto riten.**) With the tempo held back at a much slower rate of speed.

**Molto vivace** As fast and lively as possible.

**Morendo** Dying away.

**Non legato** With each note played distinctly; not slurred.

**Octave** The interval between the first and eighth tones of a major or minor scale. Octave tones share the same letter name.

**Pedal** (abbr. **ped.** or ℞.) Depress right (sustain) pedal. (See "Music Symbols")

**Pedal come sopra** (abbr. **ped. come sopra**) Use the right (sustain) pedal as previously in a similar section of the piece.

**Pedal simile** (abbr. **ped. simile** or ℞. **simile**) Pedal as previously marked.

**Pedal tenuto** (abbr. **ped. ten.**) Hold down the right (sustain) pedal.

**Più allegro** Even faster.

**Più crescendo** (abbr. **più cresc.**) Growing even louder.

**Più forte** (abbr. **più *f***) Even louder. (See "Music Symbols")

**Più lento** Even slower.

**Più moto** (also **più mosso**) With more energetic movement and speed.

**Più vivo** Even more lively and spirited.

**Poco accelerando** (abbr. **poco accel.**) A little faster.

**Poco allargando** (abbr. **poco allarg.**) Growing a little bit slower.

**Poco agitato** A little agitated.

**Poco animato** A little animated.

**Poco a poco crescendo** (abbr. **poco a poco cresc.**) Growing louder little by little.

**Poco a poco diminuendo** (abbr. **poco a poco dim.**) Growing softer little by little.

**Poco crescendo** (abbr. **poco cresc.**) Growing a little louder.

**Poco diminuendo** (abbr. **poco dim.**) Growing a little softer.

**Poco largamente** Somewhat broad and sustained.

**Poco lento e grazioso** Somewhat slowly and gracefully.

**Poco meno messo** Somewhat less loudly.

**Poco moto** With a little speed and movement.

**Poco più animato** A little more animated.

**Poco più forte** A little louder.

**Poco più mosso** A little faster.

**Poco rallentando** (abbr. **poco rall.**) A little slower.

**Poco ritardando** (abbr. **poco rit.** or **poco ritard.**) A little slower.

**Poco ritenuto** (abbr. **poco riten.**) With the tempo held back at a little slower speed.

**Poco rubato** (abbr. **poco rub.**) Somewhat freely; with prominent notes prolonged..

**Poco sostenuto** Somewhat sustained, with each note lasting nearly its full value.

**Poco slentando** Growing a little slower.

**Prestissimo** Most rapidly.

**Presto** Rapidly.

**Quasi allegretto** Almost medium fast; moderately.

**Rallentando** (abbr. **rall.**) Growing slower and slower.

**Rallentando e diminuendo** (abbr. **rall. e dim.**) Growing ever slower and softer. (See also **dimin. e rallent.**)

**Recitativo** Free in tempo and rhythm.

**Religioso** With devotion.

**R.H.** Use the right hand. (See also **L.H.**)

**Risoluto** Confidently; with vigor.

**Ritardando** (abbr. **rit.** or **ritard.**) Growing slower.

**Ritardando con grazia** (abbr. **rit. con grazia**) Growing slower with grace.

**Ritardando molto** (abbr. **rit. molto**) Growing much slower.

**Ritardando molto e dimuendo** (abbr. **rit. molto e dim.**) Growing much slower and softer.

**Ritenuto un poco** (abbr. **riten. un poco**) With the tempo held back at a little slower rate of speed.

**Ritenuto** (abbr. **riten.**) With the tempo held back at a slower rate of speed.

**Rubato.** Freely; with prominent notes prolonged.

**Sans ralentir** Without slowing the tempo.

**Scherzando** (abbr. **scherz.**) Playful.

**Secco** (abbr. **sec.**) Lightly accented; not lasting its full note value.

**Semplice** In a simple and natural manner.

**Sempre crescendo** (abbr. **sempre cresc.** or **cresc. sempre**) Growing louder throughout.

**Sempre fortissimo** (abbr. **sempre *ff*** or **sempre *fff***) Extremely loud throughout.

**Sempre legato** Smoothly throughout; with each note lasting its full value.

**Sempre più dolce** Growing sweeter throughout.

**Sempre più forte** (abbr. **sempre più *f***) Growing louder throughout.

**Sempre staccato** (abbr. **Sempre stacc.**) Lightly accented throughout, with each note lasting less than its full value.

**Senza affrettando** Without rushing.

**Senza pedal** (abbr. **senza ped.** or after a pedal marking, simply **senza**) Without pedal; release the right (sustain) pedal.

**Senza ritenuto** Without slowing down.

**Simile** In the same style as before.

**Smorzando** (abbr. **smorz.**) Fading away.

**Sostenuto** Sustained, with each note lasting its full value.

**Sostenuto con anima** Sustained and spirited, with each note lasting its full value.

**Sotto voce** As if sung softly.

**Spiritoso** Energetically; with spirit.

**Staccato** (abbr. **stacc.**) Lightly accented, with each note lasting less than its full value. (See "Music Symbols")

**Staccato il basso** (abbr. **stacc. il basso**) A lightly accented bass part; with each note lasting less than its full value.

**Staccato sempre il basso** A lightly accented bass part throughout; with each note lasting less than its full value.

**Stretto** Faster.

**Subito** (abbr. **sub.**) Suddenly, without pausing.

**Tempo di marcia** In march time.

**Tempo di valse** In waltz time.

**Tempo primo** (abbr. **Tempo I**) Return to the tempo used in the first section of the piece.

**Teneramente e grazioso** Tenderly and gracefully.

**Tenuto** (abbr. **ten.**) Sustained; with the indicated note lasting its full value or slightly longer. (See also **Sostenuto**)

**Tranquillo** Calmly.

**Tre corde** Release the left (soft) pedal.

**Très lent** Very slow.

**Trio** A second dance section in a minuet, waltz, or march, usually followed by a repeat of the first section.

**Una corda** Depress left (soft) pedal. (See "Music Symbols")

**Un poco più lento** A little more slowly.

**Un poco più ritenuto** With the tempo a little more held back; at a slightly slower rate of speed.

**Un poco ritardando** (abbr. **un poco rit.**) A little slower.

**Un poco ritenuto** (abbr. **un poco riten.**) With the tempo slightly held back; at a little slower rate of speed.

**Un poco stretto** A little faster.

**Vivace** Very fast and lively.

**Vivo** Lively and spirited.

# MUSIC SYMBOLS

## ACCENTS AND ARTICULATIONS

### Accent Marks

**fz** or **ffz**   **Forzando.** A strong, loud accent.

**fp**   **Forte piano.** A strong, loud accent which instantly diminishes to a soft volume.

**sf, sz,** or **sfz**  **Sforzando** (also **Sforzato**). A very strong, sudden, and loud accent.

**sfp**   **Sforzando piano.** A very strong, sudden, and loud accent which instantly diminishes to a soft volume

Notes marked with any of these accent signs are to be played with a strong accent and held for their full note value.

### Slurs

A curved line connecting two or more notes indicates that they should be played smoothly.

Sometimes a slur is used with staccato markings to indicate that the notes be played halfway between staccato and legato—detached, yet somewhat smooth.

### Staccato Marks

A dot above or below a note or chord indicates that it should be played with a light, crisp accent. A staccato note or chord receives less than half its indicated value.

A triangle above or below a note or chord also indicates staccato; usually with somewhat more stress.

### Ties

The tie is similar in appearance to the slur. The tie indicates that two notes of the same pitch to be played as one note value.

When two or more ties are used in sequence, the note should be held for the combined value of all tied notes.

### Phrase Mark

Like the slur, the *phrase mark* indicates that a passage be played in a smooth and connected manner. Each phrase of a piece is expressed as a distinctive musical idea, like a sentence.

## DYNAMICS

### Dynamic Marks

| | | |
|---|---|---|
| **ppp** | Pianississimo | *As soft as possible.* |
| **pp** | Pianissimo | Very soft |
| **p** | Piano | Soft |
| **mp** | Mezzo piano | Moderately soft |
| **mf** | Mezzo forte | Moderately loud |
| **f** | Forte | Loud |
| **ff** | Fortissimo | Very loud |
| **fff** | Fortississimo | As loud as possible |

### Crescendo Mark

A gradual increase in volume is indicated by a *crescendo mark.*

### Diminuendo Mark

A gradual decrease in volume is indicated by a diminuendo mark.

# O R N A M E N T S

## Grace Notes

A *grace note* is a small note that adjoins a full-sized note. Most grace notes are unaccented, and should be played as quickly as possible just before the natural beat of the note that follows.

An *accented grace note* (or *appoggiatura*) should be played as quickly as possible right on the natural beat of the attached note.

Grace notes may also occur in groups. These are usually unaccented, as shown.

## Mordents

The *upper mordent* calls for the quick alternation of the written note with the note above it.

The *lower mordent* calls for the quick alternation of the written note with the note below it.

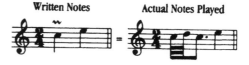

## Rolled Chords

A wavy vertical line indicates that a chord should be *rolled*. Chord tones are played one at a time in quick succession, with all notes held for the full duration of the indicated chord.

## Tremolo

A tremolo is indicated by two half notes joined together with a beam. These two pitches should each be played twice in an alternating pattern of eighth notes.

Tremolos may also be applied to other note values by adding beam marks, as shown.

## Trill

A *trill* calls for the rapid alternation of a note with the note above it. Long trills often include a wavy line after the trill sign.

# TEMPO

## Metronome Markings

The metronome is a device that taps out beats at regular intervals. It is used by musicians for setting precise tempos when practicing. Composers may indicate a precise tempo by using a *metronome marking* at the beginning of a piece or section. This indicates the note value of the basic beat and the number of beats per minute for the piece. From left to right, these metronome markings indicate *adagio, moderato, allegro,* and *presto.*

Pieces with time signatures that call for a half note, dotted quarter, or eighth note to equal one beat may include metronome markings with these notes. Each of these metronome markings indicates a moderate tempo (*moderato*).

## Fermata

The *fermata sign* (⌢) indicates that a note or chord be held for longer than its full value.

## Pause Mark

A *pause mark* (//) indicates that you stop playing briefly before continuing on.

# OTHER SYMBOLS

## Melody Line

Dotted lines are sometimes used to indicate the movement of the melody line from one hand to another, as shown.

An *octave sign* above the staff indicates that the passage be played an octave higher.

An *octave sign* below the staff indicates that the passage be played an octave lower.

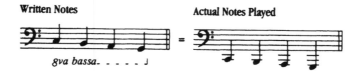

## Optional Notes

Small notes (usually in parentheses) indicate *optional notes* which should be played if possible.

## Pedal Markings

The right (sustain) pedal is the most commonly used pedal in piano music. The pedal mark (𝄢𝄡.) indicates that this pedal should be pressed. This marking (❀) is often used to indicate that the pedal should be released. Square brackets are also used to indicate when the right pedal is depressed and released, as shown.

# REPEATS AND ENDINGS

### Repeat Sign

Two dots before a double bar form a *repeat sign.* This sign is often used at the end of a piece indicating that the entire piece should be played twice.

If a *repeat sign* occurs in the middle of a piece, return to the beginning and repeat the first section before moving on.

If a mirror image of the repeat sign occurs in a composition, return to this sign when repeating the piece.

## Da Capo

D.C. is an abbreviation of the Italian phrase *Da Capo,* meaning "from the head." This marking means the same thing as a single repeat sign—repeat the piece from its beginning.

## Dal Segno

D.S. is short for the Italian phrase *Dal Segno,* meaning "from the sign." This marking means you should go back to the *dal segno sign* (𝄋) and repeat the section.

## Alternate Endings

Some compositions feature *alternate endings,* each marked with a bracket and numeral. The second time through the piece, you should skip the first ending and play the second ending.

## D.C. al Coda

This marking means you should repeat the piece until you reach the *coda sign* (⊕), then skip to the next coda sign and end the piece with the *coda* (meaning "tail").

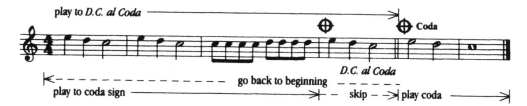

## D.S. al Coda

This marking indicates you should repeat the piece from the *dal segno sign* (𝄋). Once you reach the coda sign, skip to the next coda sign, then play the coda to end the piece.

## D.C. al Fine

*Fine* is the Italian word for "end." This marking is used in conjunction with repeat markings to indicate the point at which the piece ends. *D.C. al Fine* indicates that you should go back to the beginning of the piece and repeat until you come to the marking *Fine.*

## D.S. al Fine

*D.S. al Fine* tells you to go back to the *dal segno* sign and repeat until the point marked *Fine.*

# TABLE OF NOTES

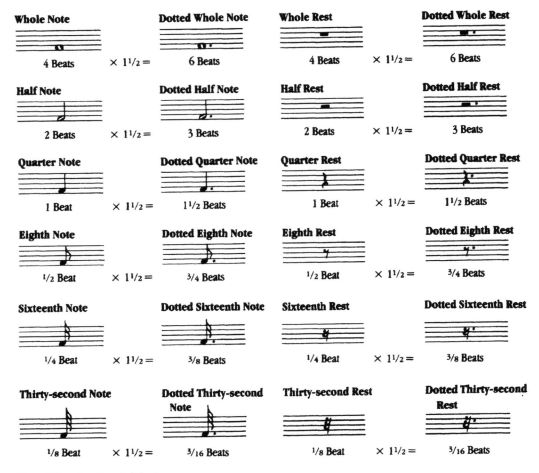

## Double-dotted Notes

A note or rest followed by two dots is worth 1¾ its normal value.

## Triplets

Three eighth-notes grouped together and marked with the numeral *3* form a triplet lasting one beat. The notes of this triplet have equal time value (each of them lasting one-third of a beat).

Three quarter notes form a triplet lasting two beats.

Here three sixteenth notes form a triplet lasting one-half of a beat and three thirty-second notes form a triplet lasting one quarter of a beat.

Here each dotted eighth note lasts one-half of a beat. Each eighth rest lasts one-third of a beat.

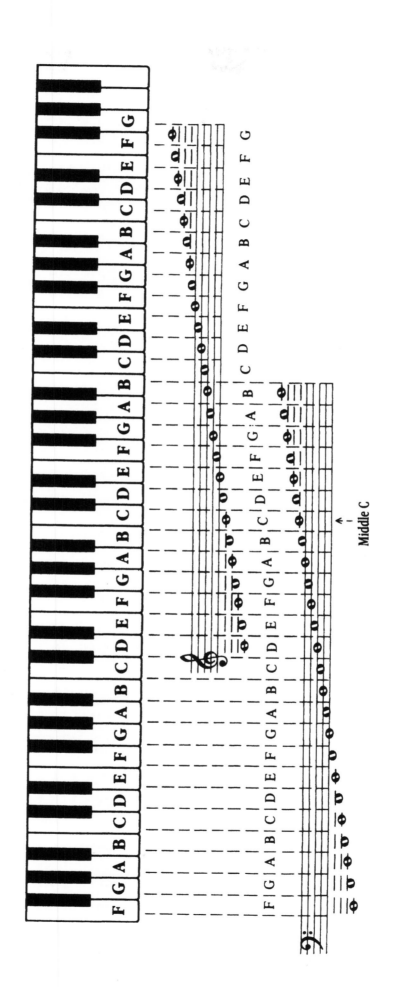

# Piano Pieces for Children 2